Return to the Promised Land

The Glorious Return of the Waldensians

By Paula Hill

Self-published by the author in February 2021

© Paula Hill 2021

Unless otherwise indicated, Scripture quotations in this publication are from the Holy Bible, King James Version.

If you have any questions about this book or about the Christian faith please contact the author via www.lausanne-english-church.com.

Cover photo: The old church tower in Bobbio Pellice

Contents

Chapter		Page
	Preface	5
1	Who were the Waldensians?	6
2	The Promised Land	9
3	Flight to Geneva	13
4	Encountering Obstacles	15
5	The Journey Begins	19
6	The Biggest Challenge	24
7	In the Promised Land	31
8	The Final Onslaught	35
9	Peace at Last	38
10	A Challenge	42
	Appendix – Waldensian statement of faith 1120	44
	Bibliography	46

Preface

In Christian circles 1689 is known as the year of publication of the Baptist Confession of Faith. However, another significant event occurred in that year that is not so well known today.

I was proofreading for Project Gutenberg when I first read the story of a small group of Waldensians, who overcame incredible odds to return to their villages in Piedmont. As a Sunday School teacher, my initial thought was that it would make a great book to give to boys, but numerous attempts to interest a publisher were unfruitful.

I read more about the Waldensians and visited the area where they lived, including the museum in Torre Pellice, which contains exhibits that relate to their history and lifestyle. On request you can see and handle their most precious possession - a copy of their Bible translated into French (the Olivetan translation of 1535). It is not an everyday item (it is huge) but its existence reminds of what was the most important thing that kept those faithful men going during the years of persecution.

May their story be a blessing to you as you read it.

Paula Hill
Montreux
Switzerland

Chapter 1

Who were the Waldensians?

The story of how in 1689 a small group of Waldensians battled through enormous challenges to regain their homeland in the mountains of Piedmont is almost unknown today in the English-speaking world, but their determination in the face of seemingly impossible odds deserves to be remembered as we give thanks to almighty God, whose eye is always upon his people. The exploits described in this account are exciting, but above all may you see how God protected his people and provided for them every step of the way.

Historians of the Reformation may mention the Waldensians in passing, but opinion is divided as to where they came from or who founded their church. Some refer to Peter Waldo, who was a travelling evangelist in the 12th century, but documents held in the library of Cambridge University which were written by the inhabitants of the valleys before 1120, predate Waldo's birth by 20 years. Beza, the early reformer, says that they originated in 120 AD, noting that their Bible was in a low form of Latin widely spoken in the 2nd century AD.

The Bible recounts the story of the birth of the early church, and at the end of the book of Acts we find the apostle Paul living in Rome and telling everyone he met the good news of salvation. We also know that before Paul was executed a faithful church had been founded in Rome, and that the letter that Paul had written them would go on to be a source of encouragement and a challenge to believers throughout the world, as it is today.

At this point the story of the first Christians in Italy becomes unclear.

History books tell us how these early believers were horribly persecuted, first by the emperor Nero and later by both secular and church leaders, even though their only crime was their determination to live faithfully in accordance with the Word of God. Because they either did not keep records or because those records have been lost, we can only find out about them and what they believed by reading the accounts of their enemies, who certainly had no desire to present them in a good light.

By the 17th century there were small groups of believers on the Italian peninsula who were living as far away from Rome as it was possible to get. If Italy is shaped like a boot then we could say that one group had journeyed South and were living in the heel in Calabria, while another group had travelled northwards from Rome and had settled in Piedmont, in the northwest corner of Italy. We can imagine how a few faithful Christians, the descendants of that first church in Rome, had gradually been forced further and further north until finally they reached the foothills of the Alps.

Once they were there, they could see the towering mountains ahead of them, which presented an almost insurmountable barrier, so they turned westwards and began looking for shelter among the surrounding hills. Imagine how they must have felt when they discovered narrow openings leading to hidden areas, where they found patches of fertile land, which in their minds' eye could be places for crops and livestock.

Hope flickered to life, as they envisaged a home where they could live in peace and remain hidden from their persecutors. And so over time they established communities, planted crops, raised their flocks and most importantly built churches where they could worship God according to his Word. For them this really did feel like the Promised Land. It did not flow with milk and honey; but with care it could provide a living.

On the lower slopes the soil was thin and rocky, which made it possible to grow vines. Because they were sheltered from the north wind by the mountains, wheat and fruit trees could be planted, and higher up rye, maize, oats, barley and potatoes as well as chestnut trees, whose nuts were a good source of protein. But in general, agriculture was only possible in about a third of the area. The rest was too high, too stony and too cold for arable farming, and the only animals that thrived were the few cows, sheep and goats who could tolerate the harsh conditions.

The men who lived this high up had to work hard to produce a crop from the rocky soil, and every animal was valued not only for the milk and meat it produced but also for the dung that could be used to enrich the soil. This was the land where the Waldensians settled and put down roots in their secret valleys. Life was not easy, they had to work hard to survive, but they were free.

Chapter 2

The Promised Land

By the 5th century AD the Roman Catholic Church had become the dominant religious force in Europe, but sadly, that church had strayed far in faith and practice from the Word of God.

The men at the head of the church grew more and more powerful and hated all those who did not submit to their absolute authority. They showed no mercy towards anybody who did not accept their teachings, especially if they used the Bible to justify their position. While they paid lip service to God's Word, they twisted the meaning of the words and added to it in such a way that the truth was lost in mixture of invention and heresy.

Services were conducted in Latin. Ordinary people who had never learned Latin, and even many of the priests had no idea what was being said. They followed meaningless rules and regulations because they had been taught that that this was the only way they could be sure of pleasing God and thereby avoid going to Hell. The Bible was both literally and spiritually a closed book for most people, which suited the Roman Catholic hierarchy very well.

But the Waldensian men and women, who lived far away from Rome in their secret communities, still loved and honoured God's word in their churches and in their lives.

In documents dated 1120 we can read their statement of faith, which makes it clear that confession should only be made to God and that it was a "diabolical doctrine" to forbid marriage to anyone.

Their translation of the Bible can still be read today, despite the fury of the Catholic church that tried to destroy it. The thought that there were ordinary people who had a version of the Bible in the vernacular, which they studied and used in their daily lives, was abhorrent to the authorities, so they increased their efforts to eradicate every one of these "heretics" and obliterate their beliefs and their churches, once and for all.

As a result, the Waldensians were no longer able to live in peace and safety. In his preface to the 1533 edition of the confession of faith of the Waldensians Martin Luther describes how, when he was a Catholic monk, he detested these people, but now praised them for their faithful adherence to the Scriptures. But during the Counter-Reformation, groups of Protestants were being persecuted and the Waldensians living in Calabria in southern Italy were exterminated.

The forces of the Pope began a long and bloody war of attrition during which Piedmont was subjected to systematic ethnic cleaning. The soldiers of the Pope would descend on the villages of the Waldensians and go about killing every person they could find. Foxe's Book of Martyrs records the lengths to which the authorities went to massacre heretics but is sufficient for us to say here that the worst atrocities we can read about in the news today reflect only part of what these faithful believers suffered in defence of their faith.

In 1603 the people of the Waldensian valleys wrote a public declaration, in which they reaffirmed their adherence to the doctrine of the apostles and the Reformed faith.

In 1655 they were forced to provide board and lodging for Catholic soldiers, ostensibly to demonstrate their allegiance to the Pope, but in reality, on Easter morning the soldiers turned on their hosts, killed them all and pillaged their meagre belongings.

Once the news of what had happened became known there was an outcry in the Protestant world, leading John Milton to write this sonnet:

> Avenge, O Lord, thy slaughtered saints, whose bones
> Lie scattered on the Alpine mountains cold;
> Even them who kept thy truth so pure of old,
> When all our fathers worshiped stocks and stones,
> Forget not: in thy book record their groans
> Who were thy sheep, and in their ancient fold
> Slain by the bloody Piedmontese, that rolled
> Mother with infant down the rocks. Their moans
> The vales redoubled to the hills, and they
> To heaven. Their martyred blood and ashes sow
> O'er all the Italian fields, where still doth sway
> The triple Tyrant; that from these may grow
> A hundredfold, who, having learnt thy way,
> Early may fly the Babylonian woe.

The Catholic church wanted to eradicate every last trace of the Waldensians, going to enormous lengths to wipe out both them and their beliefs. They even kidnapped babies and small children and put them in Catholic families so that they would not learn the truths in God's Word.

In the end it was decided that if these troublesome heretics persisted in practicing their faith despite so many of them being harassed, tortured and put to death, the only way to deal with the situation was to force them to leave Piedmont and find somewhere else to live.

Protestants in other countries, who had heard about the terrible sufferings of their brothers and sisters in Italy, did what they could to help. Oliver Cromwell, who at the time was Lord Protector of England, wrote letters on behalf of the Waldensians to the kings of Sweden and Denmark, to the united provinces of Holland and to the protestant cantons of Switzerland, and even at one point threatened military intervention. Some councillors from Amsterdam in the Netherlands chartered three ships to take people to start a new life in Delaware, USA.

Chapter 3

Flight to Geneva (1686)

One group of Waldensians from the hidden valleys of Piedmont had such a strong attachment to their "Promised Land" that they wanted to stay as close to it as they possibly could while submitting to the orders to leave their lands for good.

They decided to take up the offer of the city of Geneva, (which had been strongly Protestant since the time of Calvin) to be a city of refuge to this group of innocent believers who were facing certain death.

Geographically, Geneva is not far from Piedmont, and nowadays the two are connected by a road tunnel, but in the 17th century the Mont Blanc massif presented an almost insurmountable barrier for anyone trying to get from Italy to Switzerland. In addition to this, the Waldensians were ordered to leave immediately, even though it was the middle of winter.

We have become used to reports of streams of refugees following one another along unmarked roads towards an uncertain future, but this is not something new. The Waldensians had to leave their homes, their animals and their villages to the mercy of the soldiers of the Pope.

They knew that if they somehow managed to get to Geneva they would find fellow believers and a safe place to stay, but whether they could get there at all was another question.

They had all grown up in the foothills of the Alps and were used to picking their way along rocky tracks where the next foothold could be their last, but they knew that the towering peaks that lay between them and a place of safety presented a far greater challenge.

What was more, the order to leave did not just apply to the young and the strong. The elderly, the very sick, the new-born babies and even the heavily pregnant women had to prepare themselves for the kind of mountaineering that only someone with the right training and specialist equipment would attempt today. It is thought that of the 2,700 who set out in groups from Piedmont only 2,490 ever reached their destination, and it is not hard to imagine how many of those who died lost their footing on an icy track or just laid down for a rest and succumbed to the cold.

Those who did make it to Geneva were warmly welcomed by their Protestant brothers and sisters. Some Waldensians had anticipated the eviction and had already trekked across the Alps from Piedmont, so they were among the first to welcome the refugees. Since they had arrived in Switzerland, they had had no news from their homeland, so before long the newcomers had to answer questions about homes, livestock and above all family members who were still living in the valleys.

As more and more stories were told out about villages that had been destroyed, churches that had been taken over and the atrocities that been committed by the soldiers of the Pope, their feelings of grief and desolation grew. The precious valleys where they had built their homes, raised their children and worshipped God were now in ruins, and the likelihood of the Waldensians ever being able to return seemed to have vanished.

☐

Chapter 4

Encountering Obstacles

In the end 2,600 men, women and children arrived in Geneva. Many had not made it, but still the number left was too great for one city to accommodate them all. As time went by, they gradually spread out to other towns and villages. Some of them made their way into the south of France and even across the Atlantic to North America, but there was a group who did not want to cut their ties with Piedmont and who dreamed of one day returning to the villages they had left behind.

They could hardly bear to think about the little chapels they had built where they worshipped God and sung his praises, and the possibility that they had been destroyed, or even worse were now filled with statues and used by the Catholics for their idolatrous worship filled these men with the desire to return and reclaim their villages. Like the children of Israel in Babylon they wept when they remembered their homes and swore never to forget the land that the Lord had given them.

The Swiss wanted to help these Protestant brothers, but at the same time they were trying to keep the peace with the Duke of Savoy, who was leading the soldiers of the Pope in Piedmont. As a result, the areas around the border between Switzerland and Italy were being closely watched, not only by the soldiers of the Duke but also by the Swiss.

They did not want to risk incurring his wrath by seeming to encourage the Waldensians to return to their valleys. One small group made an abortive attempt to return, but it failed because they did not take into account the likelihood of being prevented from leaving Switzerland.

They realised that if they were going to succeed, they needed to make detailed plans and carry them out in secrecy. They settled on a route that avoided the towns and villages and instead crossed the river Rhône near where it opens out into Lake Geneva, not far from the French border. From there they planned to keep to the mountain peaks, where they would only meet a solitary shepherd or two.

Three men were chosen to go ahead, spy out the route and arrange for food dumps that could be used by others when they made their own journey, and together they decided they needed a cover story to explain their presence in case they did meet a border guard. The Waldensian women made beautiful lace, so the three men agreed that if they were questioned, they would produce some items of lace and say that they were traders looking for new markets for their products. When they set out, they must have thought about how they were following in the footsteps of Joshua and Caleb, the only difference being that they had already lived in their Promised Land and were trying to get back to it once more.

The three spies made it to Piedmont, but while they were on the return trip they met a border patrol, who recognised that they were not locals and demanded to know their business. The men produced the lace from their knapsacks, but as soon as they tried to answer questions the guards could tell that they did not have a clue about the fine fabric they were holding in their labourers' hands, so all three were arrested and thrown into prison.

On the following day they were interrogated, at which point one of the three volunteered the information that he used to be a peddler in Languedoc, in the South of France. The interrogators sent for another man who used to be involved in the same kind of work, and when he corroborated the story, the interrogators came to the conclusion that the three men were not in fact renegade Waldensians and let them go.

At this time a Frenchman called Henri Arnaud had taken the lead in the attempt to return to Piedmont. He was a pastor as well as a soldier who had a great gift for inspiring and leading his men, and the Waldensians realised that here was a man who could help them achieve their aim. While the three spies were away the message went out that an expedition was being prepared, and men started to come back from as far away as Germany. They gathered at Bex, which is a small town situated near the Rhône where the river has cut a narrow passage through the mountains.

But even though they had tried to keep their plans secret from the authorities it became known that some Waldensians were preparing to leave Switzerland and return to Piedmont. They had arranged for a boat full of arms to be sent to Villeneuve, which is at the eastern edge of Lake Geneva, but it never arrived. The chief magistrate of Aigle was obliged to call the Waldensians together and inform them that their plans were known and to forbid them to leave, which he did with tears in his eyes. Meanwhile the men who lived in the Valais, which is a Catholic canton, banded together with the men who lived in Savoy to guard St Maurice, where there is a bridge over the Rhône, to watch the river banks in case anybody tried to cross illegally.

But the political situation was unstable. The Duke of Savoy was obliged to withdraw all his troops from Savoy and the French found themselves under attack from the Dutch, meaning that they were not paying attention to what was going on in the area. Now was the time to make a third attempt to return, while everybody else was looking the other way.

By now many of the Waldensians had moved away from Geneva, so messages were sent to tell these brothers of the new plan. They needed to find a rendezvous point that was uninhabited, easy to get to, and most importantly where a large number of men could keep a low profile while they waited for everybody else to join them, and the forest at Prangins looked like the ideal spot.

The area around the motorway that runs along the northern shore of Lake Geneva, leading from Geneva in the west towards the Swiss Alps, is nowadays largely built up, but in the 17th century there were large areas of woodland, where a small army could muster and remain undetected for some time.

Prangins is situated on the opposite side of the lake from the place where the Waldensians planned begin the long march across the Mont Blanc massif, but at that moment they were just hoping that as many people as possible would be able to join them. And indeed many men left their livelihoods, their families and their homes, with no idea whether they would ever see any of them again. They had battled against both the mountains and the elements to reach a place where they were safe, but now they were prepared to risk their lives to try and reclaim their lands for the glory of God.

It was not long however before the people of Prangins noticed that something was going on in the forest. Men kept arriving, most of them on foot, but not many seemed to leave. Somebody went to find out what was going on, and before long the word began to spread; the Waldensians were making another attempt to return home. Some of the locals offered what help they could, including the use of their boats to cross the lake. This was an offer that the Waldensians were happy to accept, since not one of them had a boat of their own. They were all farmers, used to living in and near the mountains, with little experience of life on the water.

Until that point, they had concentrated on how they were going to cross the Alps, but now they realised that most of them had never handled a boat, let alone knew how to swim. The waters of Lake Geneva flow down the Rhône valley directly from the glaciers, meaning that even today a man will die if he falls in and is not rescued in time. The Waldensians would have to entrust themselves to local boatowners to help them cross the lake, and what was more they would have to make the crossing at night to avoid being spotted. Their journey was already very dangerous, even before they left Switzerland.

Chapter 5

The Journey Begins (1689)

So the slow process of transporting an army of novice sailors across western Europe's largest lake in the middle of the night began. Each boat could only take a handful of men, and there were 900 Waldensians ready to make the crossing. They knew full well that if they were all going to make it to the other side, they would need God's protection and guidance, and they also realised that the chances of every one of them disembarking in the same place seemed remote, given that the whole operation would have to be finished before dawn. The Waldensians knelt on the shore of Lake Geneva and pleaded with the One who controlled both the wind and the waves, and who had once brought his men safely to the shore, to keep them from harm as they started out on their journey home.

The first boats crossed the lake and returned for the next set of passengers, but as time went by some of the fishermen looked at the numbers still waiting and decided they could not continue. Perhaps they became afraid of discovery, or perhaps they were thinking of their own beds, but as the hours went by the number of boats diminished. Some of the Waldensians began to look up at sky. Would the sun rise and expose them on the beach before all their brothers had crossed the lake? Would they be able to find each other? And what about those who were still en route to Prangins? How many men would actually be able to join the expedition?

As the sun rose behind the mountains, they realised that, despite the difficulties and the disappointments of the night, the Lord had answered their prayers. All the Waldensians had crossed the lake and could now gather together on the same beach. As they looked around and tried to find friends and relatives, they realised that they needed to find a way of identifying each other. One of the group had had the foresight to bring with him a solution to this problem and produced from his bag a large roll of orange ribbon. Orange was the colour of Prince William of Orange, who had recently become the Protestant King of England following the Glorious Revolution, so as each man attached a strip of ribbon to his clothes, he remembered that, although they were few in number, the Waldensians were part of the great family of Protestants who were fighting the Lord's battles throughout Europe.

As they gathered together on the beach the men understood that the Lord had already blessed their journey. 900 men had embarked on fishing boats in Prangins, they had made it safely across the treacherous waters of Lake Geneva in the dead of night, and now they found themselves in the same place near the town of Yvoire as the sun came up. They fell to their knees as one man to give thanks to God for his loving protection and to ask him for his continuing presence and blessing on their journey. They not only wanted to achieve their purpose of returning to their valleys, but also they wanted to do so in a way that was God-honouring, so they decided together that for as long as they could they would pay the local farmers for any food they took and trust the Lord to supply their needs. They did not want to leave anyone with the impression that they were just a band of looters looking for their own advantage.

The people of Yvoire meanwhile had woken up to find a small army of strangers gathered just outside their town. The orange ribbons they wore told everybody that these men were Protestants, so the alarm was sounded, calling all the local farmers to come to the defence of the town. But this was a busy time in the fields; the animals needed feeding, the crops needed harvesting and the peasants had enough to do without bothering about a bunch of Protestants who had not even tried to steal any food. They felt no ill-will towards the Waldensians, so when the small army started their long march, instead of meeting any opposition they encountered local men who cheered them on and offered them parcels of food to take on their journey. When the Waldensians offered to pay for the food, they were given the locals were left with a positive impression of what it meant to be Protestant.

Despite the fact that it was now the middle of summer, the weather that day felt more like autumn. The clouds hung low over the countryside, making the road ahead hard to see, and the constant drizzling rain meant that every item of clothing the men were wearing was soon soaking wet. But worst of all, the path soon became treacherous, with loose stones and slippery mud. The Waldensians knew all about weather like this. It made their journey more difficult and dangerous, but on the other hand it meant that they were soon out of sight of anybody who might be taking an interest in the route they were taking as they disappeared into the clouds that hung over Yvoire.

As they trudged along the little army saw ahead of them a group of well-dressed men on horseback. They blocked the path and demanded to know why these strangers were on their land. However, as more and more of the Waldensians caught up with their leaders and it became clear how many men there were in this army, the mood changed and the gentlemen became more conciliatory. In fact, they were so impressed by everything that they saw and heard that they offered on the spot to write a letter of commendation that the Waldensians that could be shown to anyone who challenged them.

"These persons have arrived here to the number of 2,000 *(there were actually 900 of them)*. They have begged us to accompany them, that we may be enabled to give an account of their behaviour, which we can assure you to be perfectly reasonable. They pay for everything they take, and only require a free passage. We therefore entreat you not to sound the alarm bells, nor beat the drums, and to dismiss your men if they are under arms."

The Waldensians were grateful for this act of solidarity, but it only served to remind them that they were likely to meet plenty of others during the journey, and that not all of them would be so sympathetic. As they trudged on through the rain and the mud they knew that many challenges lay ahead, both from man and from the terrain. As they lay down and tried to sleep on that first night, many must have looked back in their minds to the hot meal and the warm bed that they had left behind.

The next day a long march lay ahead, and the men had to force themselves to forget their damp clothes and their empty stomachs and try to remember the reason for their journey. Before long they could see that the path became very narrow, with rocky cliffs rising on either side. They could also see that the path led through a town and that there was no alternative but to go through it and out the other side. Moreover the men of Cluses had obviously heard about the army of Protestants who were heading their way, and had already employed defensive measures. The gates were firmly shut, and lookouts were watching from the top of the walls. Cluses was not in the mood to welcome the Waldensians.

Henri Arnaud went up the gates of the town and started to negotiate with the inhabitants. He explained that they were peaceful people who were trying to return to the homes and land that they had lived in for generations. He assured the people of Cluses that they had no intention of doing them any harm or of stealing any property and brought forward some men who had been taken hostage the previous day. These men had shown the Waldensians the best paths to follow, and they now assured the locals that they had been well-treated.

In the end the townsfolk relented, and the Waldensian army was allowed to pass. But this time they were not greeted by cheering peasants and offers of food. Instead, the road was lined with local men, most of whom were holding a pitchfork, a gun or some other potential weapon. Their faces were grim, so the Waldensians knew that they were not welcome visitors. The little army marched through the town as quickly as possible and breathed a sigh of relief when the last man left and the gates slammed shut.

But even then the danger was not over. The path beyond Cluses ran beside the river Arve, which had been swollen by the heavy rain and now both the river and the path passed through a ravine, with towering cliffs on either side. The Waldensians were mountain men and they understood straightaway that this was a perfect place for an attack. From either side of the ravine a few men could hurl rocks down onto anyone on the track below and inflict serious injury or even death with no risk to themselves. The little army marched through the ravine as quickly as possible, with many a fearful glance towards the cliffs that surrounded them.

But they had not travelled far when they faced yet another dangerous situation. Their journey meant that they had to cross the river Arve, but ahead of them they had seen a man riding as fast as he could to give warning of their approach. When they got closer to the bridge, which was surrounded by houses, they drew up in battle formation and sent a request for safe passage to the town council. No reply came, but the Waldensians could see that several hundred men had gathered nearby, so they knew that their best option was to get across the bridge as quickly as possible and then be prepared to fight. When the locals saw what had happened, they withdrew without firing a single shot, so the Waldensians were able to continue their march.

After two days of incessant rain their clothes and shoes were soaking wet, they longed for a hot meal and a good night's sleep, but nevertheless they gave thanks to God that they had not had to fight, despite what they had faced both at Cluses and at the bridge over the Arve. A peaceful night was what they all needed because the next day they knew they were going to face their biggest challenge yet.

Chapter 6

The Biggest Challenge

Between the Waldensians and their homeland lay a formidable barrier. The Mont Blanc massif stretches along the borders between Switzerland, France and Italy and contains eleven major summits including Mont Blanc, which is the highest peak in Western Europe. These mighty mountains are covered in snow, and glaciers of varying sizes are a common feature of the landscape.

The Waldensians had already faced part of this perilous journey once when they were forced to leave their homes and seek refuge in Geneva. That had happened in the middle of winter when conditions were at their cruellest, but even though it was now summertime they knew that what lay ahead of them would be just as dangerous as it had been in winter, when every step they took could lead to a slip, a slide and a fall onto the jagged rocks below.

We now know that during the 17th century the Alps went through a mini-ice age, making the weather very cold even in summertime. The route they were following meant that they would have to cross the mountain range in an area that consisted of a series of peaks and valleys, which would take their toll on legs that were already tired after three days' hiking. They knew that the paths were so slippery and the surfaces so unstable that they would often have to resort to sitting down and sliding to the bottom of the slopes. They had no protective clothing, no specialist climbing boots and the only food they had with them was milk and cheese.

But when they looked up to the mountains that lay ahead of them, they reminded themselves of the words of Psalm 121, which declares that the God they worshipped was the one who had made the mountains, and that he could and would watch over them and take them back to the valleys they had left behind.

> I will lift up mine eyes unto the hills, from whence cometh my help.
>
> My help cometh from the Lord, which made heaven and earth.
>
> He will not suffer thy foot to be moved: he that keepeth thee will not slumber.
>
> Behold, he that keepeth Israel shall neither slumber nor sleep.
>
> The Lord is thy keeper: The Lord is thy shade upon thy right hand.
>
> The sun shall not smite thee by day, nor the moon by night.
>
> The Lord shall preserve thee from all evil: he shall preserve thy soul.
>
> The Lord shall preserve thy going out and thy coming in from this time forth, and even for evermore.

On the face of it even the weather seemed to against them. The low clouds and persistent rain continued, making the rocky paths even more treacherous and reducing visibility to a few paces. However, the Waldensians took comfort from the thought that if they had difficulty finding the way ahead then anybody who was trying to follow them would also find it hard to work out exactly where they were.

And so their journey continued, up one peak and down the other side. Their clothes and their shoes became more and more threadbare and offered little protection against the rain, which turned into snow as they gradually ascended higher and higher.

One evening they found some shepherds' huts and crawled gratefully inside, until one man suggested that they used the wood from the roofs to make a fire. The thought of heat and light was so appealing that the men stripped the wood from the roofs without thinking, and it was not until they were huddled around their pitiful fires, whose sodden wood gave off as much smoke as they did heat, that they realised that they had just burnt the only protection they had against the snow. The army slept very badly that night, even though they gathered together to share what body heat they had left.

In the morning they woke to face another day of struggling through heavy snow in wet clothes, with little to fill their stomachs to give them strength for the journey. And so they battled on, knowing that every painful step brought them closer to their destination. More than once they met with opposition, as local men banded together to try and prevent their passage, but on every occasion the Lord was with them and enabled them to carry on.

There were times when the path was not so challenging, and then one of the men would start to sing and the others would join in. But these were not traditional marching songs. Instead the Waldensians loved to sing the hymns of praise like this, which they used to enjoy singing in the chapels of Piedmont:

> For the strength of the hills we bless Thee,
> Our God, our father's God!
> Thou hast made thy children mighty
> By the touch of the mountain sod.
>
> Thou hast fixed our ark of refuge
> Where the spoiler's foot ne'er trod;
> For the strength of the hills we bless Thee,
> Our God, our father's God!

Their spirits lifted as they sang the words that they loved so well, remembered the Promised Land that lay ahead of them and were reassured that their God would give them victory over everything that stood in their way.

So far the Waldensians had not had to use the few weapons that they had with them, even though the authorities knew who they were and what they were trying to do. But as men approached the bridge at Salabertrand, which was the only way forward, they were faced with an army of 2,200 French soldiers, all armed and ready to prevent the little army from getting any further.

With rocks on one side of the path and the river on the other they had no choice. As they approached, the bridge the cry rang out "Who's there?", to which they replied "Friends", because they still hoped pass by in peace. But the French soldiers had no intention of letting these rebels through, and their response was immediate and violent. The cry went up "Kill, kill!", followed by a hail of gunfire that lasted for 15 minutes.

At the first shot Henri Arnaud ordered all his men to lie flat on the ground. However, some of them were obliged to defend themselves against two companies of French soldiers who attacked them from the rear, so they were caught in a pincer movement. When the firing ceased the command was given to get up and take the bridge, and the Waldensians knew that this was a critical moment. When somebody called out "Courage, the bridge is won!" they rushed forward with every weapon they had at the ready. The fighting was fierce, but after it was over the little army, who between them had virtually no experience of war, looked around in amazement.

They were all exhausted after the gruelling journey that had brought them to this point and yet they had managed to defeat an army of 2,500 trained soldiers, not to mention those who had attacked them in the rear. In their determination to take the bridge some of them had rushed upon the enemy even as they were about to fire and had taken them so much by surprise that they had not pulled the trigger.

In all about 15 Waldensians had been killed and 12 injured but those who had survived were able to look back at the bridge and realise that God alone had granted them a famous victory. As they collected all the food and the weapons that their adversaries had dropped, their hearts were filled with rejoicing, despite their fatigue.

But there was no time to lose. The Waldensians knew that they could not rest, even though the only thing they wanted to do was to lie down and sleep. Their leaders went around urging each man to get ready to march on, but for a few this was beyond their powers. They stayed where they were, and so they were captured by the enemy and never reached their homeland. But for those who managed to drag themselves upright and keep on marching the next day brought them in sight of the mountains they had been longing to see. It was the Lord's day, and when they saw the familiar peaks of their homeland, they fell to their knees to give thanks to God for bringing them safe thus far.

Just one more rocky slope to slide down, just one more cliff face to scramble up and then the Waldensians found themselves standing on the edge of their Promised Land. Eleven days earlier 900 men had crossed Lake Geneva. Since then they had faced many challenges, from extreme weather to violent opposition, but by God's grace they had survived and now stood ready to retake their lands. They knew that many more difficulties lay ahead of them, but their spirits rose and they faced the future with renewed confidence.

Of the 900 men who had started the expedition about 700 remained. Some had had been killed, some had been overcome by the cold, a few had deserted and those who remained realised that they would need to manage what resources they had with extreme care. In the course of their journey they had taken a few hostages with experience of the massif, and it was with reluctance that these men were now killed. This was the first time that the Waldensians had committed such an act.

The little army marched further into the valleys that they knew so well. They were constantly on the alert for enemy attack, either from the rear or ahead of them, because they knew that the soldiers of the Duke of Savoy had been mustered to prevent them retaking their homeland, but every step was a delight because they were following paths that led to fields and villages that they knew so well.

Everywhere they could see evidence of the damage that had already been caused by the Catholic soldiers, so when they arrived in the village of Guigot to find that the church still standing they opened the door with some trepidation. And their fears were realised – the little chapel had obviously been used as a place of worship by the Catholic soldiers and now contained idols and other objects that had been used in their ceremonies.

The Waldensians lost no time in removing every sign of idolatry from the building. They built a large bonfire outside and threw all the detestable objects in the flames.

Then all 700 of them crowded into the building and together sang a hymn of praise to their God, who had enabled them to reclaim this place of worship.

> Hast Thou cast us off forever?
> Will Thine anger no more cease?
> Shall Thy people never, never
> Dwell again, O Lord, in peace?
> Oh, behold the desolation!
> See Thy holy place defiled!
> Scattered is Thy congregation,
> And Thy sanctuary spoiled.
>
> Rise, O Lord, in might victorious,
> Rise and give Thy people aid;
> Come, O come in triumph glorious,
> Overwhelm Thy foes dismayed.
> Circled with a thousand wonders,
> Girt with all Thy power and strength,
> Mid ten thousand thousand thunders
> Save, redeem Thy own, at length!

As Henri Arnaud got up to preach, he reminded the men of the last pastor in the area, who had been martyred for his faith not far from where the little army was standing. Every man who was present remembered that they were fighting for the truth in the heart of enemy territory, as they looked to Almighty God for his care and protection.

As they set off again and continued their march further into their own valleys the Waldensians were always on the alert for any signs of the soldiers of the Pope. This was familiar territory for them – they could easily identify positions that offered the enemy a place to attack and so kept well away from them, but they were also keenly aware that because there were so few of them would have to be extra careful because of the size of the formidable army that was determined to exterminate them.

As they were approaching the village of San Guiliano they heard voices calling to them from beyond the closed gates. "Come on, varlets of the devil, we occupy all the passes, and there are 3,000 of us!"

The Waldensians knew that because they were heavily outnumbered, their best option was to attack immediately and take the enemy by surprise. They charged the gates with such violence that the men of San Guiliano were completely overwhelmed, and before long the Waldensians had achieved another remarkable victory. In fact their attack was so successful that only one of their soldiers was killed in the battle, and before long they were able to stand inside the gates and gather together all the weapons that their opponents had been using against them.
☐

Chapter 7

In the Promised Land

The Waldensians were in their Promised Land, but just like the children of Israel they knew that it was still under the control of their enemies and that their small army would have to stay completely united if it was to be victorious. They took the town of Bobbio and the following day held a service of thanksgiving for the Lord's provision and protection. They also spent some time appointing a mayor and other officials, so that all their affairs could be administered fairly, including the distribution of any booty. At the end of the day they gathered together to take a solemn oath, which they swore to God and to each other.

"God, by His divine grace, having happily re-conducted us to the inheritance of our fathers, there to establish the pure service of our holy religion, ... we, pastors, captains, and other officers, swear and promise before the face of the living God, ... neither to separate nor disunite while God grants us life, even should we have the misfortune to be reduced to three or four.... And to the intent that union, which is the soul of our affairs, should remain inviolable among us, the officers shall swear fidelity to the soldiers, and the soldiers to the officers, promising together to our Lord and Saviour Jesus Christ to deliver, if possible, our brethren from the cruel woman of Babylon, and with them to re-establish and maintain his kingdom till death, and observe all our lives with good faith this present ordinance."

The Waldensians knew that their opponents had more soldiers, more weapons and certainly more training than they had had. They were just a group of men who were following a path that they believed God wanted them to follow to the end, and like David they had every confidence that he would give them the victory, even though the odds seemed to be stacked against them. Their numbers were gradually dwindling, as one by one men were lost in battle or became ill due to their poor diet. Sometimes all they could find to eat was a few vegetables or a handful of nuts, although on one occasion they were able to harvest a field of wheat and grind it in the local mill. They also raided their enemies' convoys and captured valuable food supplies, which they took and stored for future use.

Some Frenchmen had been with the Waldensians during this long and weary journey, but one of their leading men whose name was Turel, lost heart during this time. He was a leading figure, and he persuaded four of his compatriots to follow him. They left the little army because they saw no hope of success and feared death by slow starvation, but Turel was captured by their enemies and, strapped to a wheel while still alive and died a horrible death. This was the way that the forces of the Roman Catholic church dealt with anybody who opposed them.

Even though there were only a few hundred Waldensians soldiers left, the Duke of Savoy continued to send reinforcements to dislodge them once and for all from their hideaways in the mountains and bring to a conclusion his extermination programme.

During the autumn of 1689 increasing numbers of Piedmontese and French soldiers began to appear in the valleys, so that eventually nearly every village was occupied. Some of the Waldensians became fearful and deserted, but they were soon captured and killed. The noose was tightening as the survivors faced an army twenty times its size; they realised that they needed to take action and take it fast. They held a war council during which various suggestions were made, but each man had his own opinion and discussion began to descend into conflict. Just in time Henri Arnaud stood up and took control. He suggested that they take the matter to the Lord in prayer and immediately began to pray. He then suggested that the Waldensians make their way to Balsiglia where the rocks rise out of thick woodland into natural terraces above a raging torrent, thus providing natural barrier to any attack. The decision was taken and that same night they gathered together everything they owned and made their way to Balsiglia.

In some places the path was so steep that they had to scramble up on their hands and knees, but when they made it to the top they began to make the most of their position. They built entrenchments, walls and watercourses and dug dwellings for themselves out of the earth. They found the millstone that had been abandoned when the last resident left Balsiglia and were able to get it to work, since their intention was to make this place their home for the time being.

Every day Henri Arnaud led the Waldensians in prayer before they went to work on making their camp as secure as possible. They improved the natural features of the area so that if an enemy attacked on one level they could retreat to the terrace above and so on until the summit was reached, where they also built a fort and a lookout post which was manned at all times. For the time being they could sit back and wait for their enemies to act.

Eventually the Duke of Savoy became of tired of this game of cat and mouse and decided to launch one more attack in an attempt to dislodge the Waldensians from their eyrie. He mustered 4,000 men in the valley below and armed them with guns and cannon.

The little army was now only 300 men strong and as they looked down from their positions on the hillside they could see that they were hopelessly outnumbered in terms of manpower and weapons. But despite all this they knew, just as David did when he faced Goliath, that they had Almighty God on their side and that he was greater than any enemy. In the early hours of the morning the Duke's soldiers were woken by the sound of singing floating down from the peaks above their heads. The Waldensians were singing Psalm 68:

> Let God arise, let His enemies be scattered:

> Let them also that hate Him flee before Him.

> As smoke is driven away, so drive them away:

> As wax melteth before the fire,
>
> So let the wicked perish.

As they listened the Duke's soldiers laughed. This was not a confident battle hymn, sung by men who were certain of victory. They could tell from their voices that the Waldensians were few in number and had been weakened by the time that they had spent deprived of sleep and proper meals. This fight was going to be short, brutal and easily won, or so they thought.

Chapter 8

The Final Onslaught

The following morning the two armies made their preparations. The Catholic soldiers loaded and primed their guns and were about to take to the field when they looked up. What was that falling from the sky? The flurry of white flakes could surely not be snow, could it? After all, this was the month of May, so it would not last for long. But instead of petering out the snow became heavier and heavier and soon it was settling on the ground and covering everything in sight. It carried on falling, so that the soldiers could hardly see where they were going, let alone work out where their opponents were. Meanwhile the Waldensians gave thanks to God for sending the snow. Life in the valleys had taught them from an early age the easiest way to get around during a snowstorm, so now they were able to use this experience to gain any advantage they could.

After some time, when they had made no advance at all, the commander of the Catholic army decided to bring his heavy artillery into the battle. This consisted of a huge cannon on wheels which had to be manoeuvred into position so that it could shell the enemy. In certain conditions this was just a matter of moving the cannon across a field, but this battle was taking place on a rocky mountainside, so the soldiers had to somehow drag their cast iron cannon up a steep track and wedge into a position where they could target the Waldensians and do all this in the middle of a snowstorm.

When they finally got the cannon into place they loaded it ready for firing. It didn't take long for the Waldensians to realise that the enemy was using a weapon against which they had no defence, even with all their experience and abilities. They had no choice but to leave their positions and scramble higher up the mountainside, out of range of the cannon. As the sun set the last remnants of the little army looked down from their hiding place onto their beloved valleys and wondered what the next day would bring. The French commander of the Duke's troops was so confident of victory that he sent a message to Paris announcing that the Waldensians had been destroyed.

Nobody slept well that night, and in the morning the men were able to see that the Lord had sent them even more challenging weather. Not only could they not see the enemy with their formidable cannon, but also they could hardly make out the man standing next to them because of the heavy fog that had descended during in the night. The combination of poor visibility and snow underfoot made moving around even more difficult, and their only consolation was that they knew that their enemy was finding the situation just as difficult as they were.

However, as the Waldensians looked around them they realised that the heavy fog offered them a way out of their predicament. They were so familiar with the area that they knew that it was possible to get from the mountain where they were seemingly trapped to another peak, where they would be out of reach of the enemy and their cannon. To get there they would have to pick their way along a narrow and treacherous path, so they would have to watch every step that they took. It was not really a path at all, but some of them had used it when trying to rescue a lost sheep or hunt a mountain goat, and most importantly it now offered them a way of escape.

The heavy fog meant that if they managed to leave silently and make no sound en route they could get away from their enemy without any of them becoming aware that their prey was escaping. The Waldensians proceeded to dismantle their makeshift camp in absolute silence. Every weapon and cooking pot was wrapped up, and every man made sure that none of his equipment could clank and alert the enemy. Then each man set out on the most hazardous journey they had ever undertaken.

The fog had reduced the visibility to a few feet, and the snow on the ground made every step treacherous, but the Waldensians used all the agility they had acquired over the years to creep away in silence. Some of the enemy were asleep, others were sitting around their campfires waiting for the fog to lift and the sun to rise, but even though their prey passed quite close to them not one of them heard any noise and raised the alarm.

When it began to get light and the fog cleared the Duke's soldiers looked up, expecting to see their opponents cowering at the top of the mountain. But to their amazement there was nobody in sight. What was more there was no sound coming from their camp nor any sign of activity. Eventually some soldiers climbed up to find out was going on, but discovered that the Waldensians had disappeared, leaving only a few extinguished campfires behind them.

Meanwhile the little army had managed to escape from their eyrie and had scrambled their way up another peak some distance away and out of range. As the fog finally cleared they looked back at the way they had come and their hearts failed them – had they really managed to make that journey in silence, without a single one of them falling to their death?

Now they could see how difficult and dangerous the track was, and yet they had all reached their destination safely. Surely the Lord had been with them. He had sent the snow and then the fog, and he had guarded his people through many dangers as they fled to safety. What a wonderful example of his loving provision.

Chapter 9

Peace at Last

There seemed to be no end in sight in this deadly game of hide and seek, with the French army chasing the Waldensians from one mountain hideaway to another until the last one of them was killed, but God, who had already demonstrated how he controlled the weather, now showed that his power is far greater than that of the greatest earthly ruler, and that even the heart of the king is in his hands, as Proverbs 21:1 tells us.

For years the Duke of Savoy had been trying to exterminate the Waldensians because he was in an alliance with the Catholic King of France, but for some time recently he had been in negotiation with the Protestants, and shortly after the escape from Balsiglia, he decided to break his treaty with France and ally himself instead with England and Austria. This meant that he was now friends with the allies of the Waldensians and that they in turn were no longer his enemies.

He ordered his troops to stop hunting them down, and as a result the valleys of Piedmont were left in peace for a time. The men came down from the mountains and began to rebuild their homes and churches and life become almost normal again.

The persecution did not stop completely, and for years the Waldensians were harassed by their Catholic neighbours. Many of them finally emigrated and went to live in Protestant countries, but they were never again forced to abandon completely their valleys. Even though we have no records to prove it we can assume that in time some of the women and children came back to Piedmont to join their husbands and fathers. Now whole families could meet for worship, read their Bibles and follow its commandments without the constant threat of persecution hanging over them.

Their descendants are still living in the valleys of Piedmont, which is the only part of Italy where half the population are Protestants. Visitors today can see churches that call themselves Waldensian and discover the places where their forefathers hid from their enemies and fought to survive. However, they will also find that the churches are now liberal and ecumenical, and the noticeboards advertise services conducted by women. The Wikipedia entry for the modern Waldensian church makes reference to its toleration of homosexuality, which would have been abhorrent to those early believers.

In the museum where the Waldensians celebrate their history there are many interesting exhibits, including artefacts which show how they used to live. The library has a copy of their own translation of the Bible written in 17th century French. But there is also a chart on the wall that indicates all the places of worship in the area and this chart includes not only Catholic churches, but also the local mosque and the Kingdom Hall of the Jehovah Witnesses! The churches even take pride in the fact that they work with the Roman Catholics and accept their beliefs and practices, even though their ancestors suffered and died at the hands of soldiers who were loyal to the Pope.

The way that the Waldensians overcame seemingly insurmountable obstacles to recover their homeland is known in Italian as Il Glorioso Rimpatrio, or the Glorious Return. We have drawn comparisons between what they did to the return of the children of Israel to the Promised Land and looking at what happened next will help us understand how their story is relevant to us in the 21st century.

The Israelites knew that they were going to be living in enemy territory, and the Lord had warned them not to have anything to do with the Canaanites or with their idolatry (Deuteronomy 7). The Waldensians were also living among idolaters, and initially they set about destroying every sign of their presence.

But the Bible tells us that after their return to the Promised Land the Israelites did not manage to destroy the Canaanites. By the time Joshua was an old man we can read about how they were not able to completely eradicate the Canaanites from the land, beginning with Jerusalem and carrying on from tribe to tribe (Joshua 15 onwards).

It is not hard to imagine that the same kind of thing happened in the Waldensian valleys. After all, they lived in the same area as many Catholics, and would have met each other in the fields and the marketplaces. Children grow up and want to get married, and unless they really grasp how important it is for believers to only marry fellow believers the next generation will be influenced by the beliefs and lifestyle of their husbands and wives. Over time, even faithful Christians are affected by what they see and hear around them, and unless they protect themselves by constantly going back to God's Word, they will gradually become more and more worldly.

The story of the Waldensians is a challenging one for us. We read about the way that they tackled and overcame massive challenges by God's grace and were prepared to suffer and die for the truth on a daily basis, and we are impressed. But we ask ourselves, would we be as brave and show as much perseverance as they did if we faced a similar challenge today?

From the comfort of our centrally heated homes, with numerous Bibles and Christian books on our shelves and plenty of food in the kitchen we find it hard to imagine a life where these things have been taken away. And yet we know that for many Christians today even the next meal is uncertain, and the word of God is something that they have in their hearts, not in their hands. We take so much for granted and lose sight of what is really important. If a stranger came into our homes would they be able to tell straightaway the Lord was the head of the house? Is there anything about our daily lives that sets us apart from our neighbours except for the fact that we go to church on Sundays?

We could argue that for the Waldensians the Glorious Return was their spiritual high point. They had had to depend on God and see his provision for them for every step they took and every bite they ate. But when the persecution died down and they had the freedom to live their lives in the way they wanted to, they gradually got out of the habit of trusting the Lord for everything. As a result his Word became less and less important in their daily lives and they stopped looking to it for guidance and support in every situation.

Because they no longer had to fight for what they knew to be right but could relax and enjoy God's good gifts, they got out of the habit. Just like the children of Israel, who never managed to drive the Canaanites out of the Promised Land and instead became more and more like their neighbours, the Waldensians lost their absolute obedience to God and his word and started to conform to the world around them.

As we look back on their story, let us resolve not to let the same thing happen to us.

☐

Chapter 10

A Challenge

In the 19th century a Waldensian pastor wrote a book detailing their history. In it he refers to them as the Vaudois, which is the French name for the Waldensians. This is how it ends.

A WORD

TO MY DEAR FELLOW-COUNTRYMEN OF THE VAUDOIS VALLEYS.

Having now reached the termination of the History of the Vaudois Church from its origin, and of the Vaudois of the Valleys of Piedmont to the present day, I cannot take my leave of you, for whom principally I have written this work, without addressing a parting word. It is that of an old man, known to all your pastors, the greater part of whom have been his pupils, and of whom more than one are his kinsmen. I may then say to all of you, as Abraham to Lot, "Are we not brethren?" Listen then to my voice.

The corner of the earth that you inhabit, under the vault of heaven and the inspection of the Omnipotent, has been from time immemorial the cradle of our Vaudois church. Our origin, as evangelical Christians, goes back to the first ages of the Christian church. It has been attempted to brand with ridicule that just claim which constitutes our glory. Error has endeavoured to forge a false history for you. As a son of the martyrs, like yourselves, as a descendant of the most ancient confessors of the truth, I have felt it my duty to retrace the facts for you, to place before your eyes the testimonies on which our history rests; I have done it without art, guided as I have been by the love of the truth.

Ye descendants of the Vaudois, aspire to resemble your forefathers. Ye have received from generation to generation the glorious heritage of sound doctrine; transmit it, unimpaired, to your children. In your retired valleys, as in the days of darkness, the Eternal has preserved the light which was extinguished elsewhere; guard it carefully, now that it shines with renovated splendour in other places and in other climes. To faith in the Father, Son and Holy Spirit join the proof of your sincerity; a life of renunciation of sin, of entire devotedness to your heavenly Shepherd, to the Sovereign Redeemer of your souls! "Let your light so shine before men, that they may see your good works, and glorify your Father, which is in heaven."

But for this end, dear fellow-countrymen, guard against saying with self-complacency, like the church of Laodicea, "I am rich, and increased with goods, and have need of nothing." Dread lukewarmness and religious indifference – for behind these faults, death lies in ambush. The life of the soul which, as well as that of the body, God alone gives, equally requires nourishment. Give it the nourishment that suits it, and it will live. Jesus is the Bread of Life – seek for him in your Bible, by continual reading; seek for him in heaven, by your prayers; seek for him in the church, which is his body, by associating with the faithful, with assembled saints, and by approaching with faith and repentance the table of the Lord.

Dear fellow countrymen! I now take my leave of you and your families, imploring on your persons as I do on this work, the Divine blessing.

> Your Brother in the faith, as well as in the flesh,
> ANT. MONASTIER,
> Pastor

Lausanne,
Oct. 13, 1846

Appendix

The Waldensians' statement of faith (circa 1120)

1. We believe and firmly maintain all that is contained in the twelve articles of the symbol, commonly called the apostles' creed, and we regard as heretical whatever is inconsistent with the said twelve articles.

2. We believe that there is one God – the Father, Son, and Holy Spirit.

3. We acknowledge for sacred canonical scriptures the books of the Holy Bible. *(Here follows the title of each, exactly conformable to our received canon, but which it is deemed, on that account, quite unnecessary to particularize).*

4. The books above-mentioned teach us: That there is one GOD, almighty, unbounded in wisdom, and infinite in goodness, and who, in His goodness, has made all things. For He created Adam after His own image and likeness. But through the enmity of the Devil, and his own disobedience, Adam fell, sin entered into the world, and we became transgressors in and by Adam.

5. That Christ had been promised to the fathers who received the law, to the end that, knowing their sin by the law, and their unrighteousness and insufficiency, they might desire the coming of Christ to make satisfaction for their sins, and to accomplish the law by Himself.

6. That at the time appointed of the Father, Christ was born – a time when iniquity everywhere abounded, to make it manifest that it was not for the sake of any good in ourselves, for all were sinners, but that He, who is true, might display His grace and mercy towards us.

7. That Christ is our life, and truth, and peace, and righteousness – our shepherd and advocate, our sacrifice and priest, who died for the salvation of all who should believe and rose again for their justification.

8. And we also firmly believe that there is no other mediator, or advocate with God the Father, but Jesus Christ. And as to the Virgin

Mary, she was holy, humble, and full of grace; and this we also believe concerning all other saints, namely, that they are waiting in heaven for the resurrection of their bodies at the day of judgment.

9. We also believe, that, after this life, there are but two places – one for those that are saved, the other for the damned, which [two] we call paradise and hell, wholly denying that imaginary purgatory of Antichrist, invented in opposition to the truth.

10. Moreover, we have ever regarded all the inventions of men [in the affairs of religion] as an unspeakable abomination before God; such as the festival days and vigils of saints, and what is called holy-water, the abstaining from flesh on certain days, and such like things, but above all, the masses.

11. We hold in abhorrence all human inventions, as proceeding from Antichrist, (*Alluding probably to the voluntary penances and mortification imposed by the Catholics on themselves*) which produce distress and are prejudicial to the liberty of the mind.

12. We consider the Sacraments as signs of holy things, or as the visible emblems of invisible blessings. We regard it as proper and even necessary that believers use these symbols or visible forms when it can be done. Notwithstanding which, we maintain that believers may be saved without these signs, when they have neither place nor opportunity of observing them.

13. We acknowledge no sacraments [as of divine appointment] but baptism and the Lord's supper.

14. We honour the secular powers, with subjection, obedience, promptitude, and payment.

Bibliography

A History Of The Vaudois Church: From Its Origin And Of The Vaudois Of Piedmont To The Present Day (1848). Antoine Monastier

The Vaudois of Piedmont: A visit to their valleys, with a sketch of their remarkable history as a church and people to the present date. N. Worsfold, M.A. (1873)

The History of the Evangelical Churches of the Valleys of Piemont (sic). (1658) Samuel Morland. Forgotten Books (2018 reprint)

The Israel of the Alps: A history of the persecutions of the Waldenses. Alexis Muston. Tentmaker Publications 2003

Printed in Great Britain
by Amazon

29261667R00030